Elevating Purpose

Elevating Purpose
Streams of Promise *Volume I*

LaDonna Booker-McLemore

AuthorHouse™
1663 Liberty Drive
Bloomington, IN 47403
www.authorhouse.com
Phone: 1-800-839-8640

Published by AuthorHouse   02/13/2015

ISBN: 978-1-4969-4438-2 (sc)
ISBN: 978-1-4969-7276-7 (e)

Library of Congress Control Number: 2014917906

Print information available on the last page.

Contents

Poetry Compilation

DEDICATION

This book is dedicated to my two beautiful young adults, Jamil and LaT'elle Booker. Without you guys being my children, I would have given up on life. LaT'elle, I recall when you were younger seeing the strength that you possess gave me strength, and I became resilient. You're a helping hand, intelligent and your courage encouraged me in silence.

To my beautiful son, Jamil, the essence of your strength has been a reflection of God. I've always known the love you have for me and I pray this book helps you on your spiritual journey. The desire to become a better person and mother for my children led me to a relationship with Jesus Christ. With that being said, teaching them about God was important. As I look back, all I can say is that the Most High blessed me with two beautiful, amazing, talented children that led me to the place I'm in today. I've made plenty of mistakes as a young parent with very little guidance. My sincere apology and love to you all.

ACKNOWLEDGMENTS

With sincere thanks, I acknowledge Bishop Mariea Claxton, for displaying true righteousness. Elevating Purpose wouldn't be possible without her steadfast teachings over the course of fifteen years. I greatly appreciate Bishop for counsel when things were bleak. Bishop is a profound leader and a spiritual mother. Bishop's ministry speaks volumes of unconditional love and truth.

I've been challenged to accept love and to have confidence in my ability as a writer/poet.

With sincere thanks, I acknowledge Pure Hope Ministries, for accepting me; especially, when I was a complete wreck. Pure Hope has expressed unity on a greater level like none I've ever seen.

Pure Hope teaches leadership to all. We're on a spiritual quest as one mind being catapulted in our relationship as the Sons of God. Elevating Purpose represents the seed that blossomed from Bishop Mariea and Pure Hope. I would like to sincerely thank Lorna Jackie Wilson for her guidance and creativity in support of the completion of my book.

Last but not least, I acknowledge my husband, Harold McLemore III. I sincerely thank you for your support, faith, love and encouragement. You have seen all of my visions and never gave up on my pursuit of my dream as an entrepreneur.

FOREWORD

We are all on a journey and for most of us, our journey began with years of hurt, pain, disappointment, and fear. We've been to church, heard the sermons, and even remembered a verse or two of our favorite scripture. But at some point, our spirit begins to desire more. It yearns for truth and love so the real journey begins. Through nights of praying and crying out to the Lord in the "darkness," the seed begins to germinate.

"Faith as a grain of mustard seed," is what the Bible says, will move mountains. The power of spoken words can incite change in our lives that will give us the courage to continue on this journey. Taking these "tiny" steps of faith, accepting love, and renewing our minds is paramount in our transformation and deliverance. When we examine ourselves and release the past, then the seed can bloom.

The author of these potentially life-changing poems, LaDonna "Lady" McLemore is a prophetess with wisdom and vision beyond her imagination. She has a thirst for truth and righteousness with a relentless passion for the Kingdom of God. LaDonna McLemore is a gift from God and a jewel in the earth, and I firmly believe all who read Elevating Purpose shall receive wisdom, knowledge, and revelation. Through the most powerful gift, i.e., love, Elevating Purpose empowers all to go forth in faith, declaring the bountiful blessings of God over their lives.

This progressively elevating book with its attention-grabbing flow affirms the love and creativity that our loving Father God has for all His Sons. LaDonna has lovingly presented this gift to the world by allowing God to speak through her in a very transparent and honest way. This book will help to challenge, confront, and change those areas of our lives holding us in bondage.

I am one of a host of people who have been inspired by LaDonna's prophetic writings. So, be prepared to have your spirit awakened.

Darlene D. McDaniel

PREFACE

Elevating Purpose didn't begin as a book. I was enjoying my new discovery for writing poetry.

Then GOD spoke to me saying, "I would write several books of poetry." This began in 2002. Elevating Purpose are poems of my spiritual journey. The importance of this book addresses the deep rooted issues that people don't want to acknowledge or face. Elevating Purpose exposes the obscurity embedded within one's self.

In my journey I've advanced as a poet, mother, and mainly as a woman. I was motivated by several events as well as people. On this spiritual quest, I've been challenged and tested daily. My growing pains allowed me to pursue newness on a smaller scale. This compilation of poetry is not the typical. Yet, it is the prophetic, spoken from my spirit. It is the voice of the Divine Mind. It is the truth that addresses daily issues of life.

INTRODUCTION

This is the journey of a young lady that was lost with no self-worth. This void or emptiness, if you will evoked a deep search for love. At the age of six, I recall contemplating suicide due to my environment. Depression and lack of faith eventually overcame my mind.

My mother was addicted to drugs and her ability to care for my siblings and I withered away. The mental, verbal and physical abuse affected me emotionally. The thoughts of abandonment caused me to isolate from my family. As a teenager, living in the inner city with no guidance, lack and fear led me down the path of becoming a mother at seventeen.

With no hope, looking for dysfunctional love became the norm. Eventually, chaos and sexual abuse consumed me, resulting in a nervous breakdown at twenty one. That experience compelled me to start seeking God on a greater scale. I wanted freedom, love and deliverance.

I had to conquer the mindset that I allowed to destroy me for most of my life. Writing poetry has been a tool for me to release, express and address all trauma that occurred. This allowed me to hear my spirit in an unimaginable way. God has truly shown me that by applying the principle of thinking positively; it can change one's life. Elevating Purpose is one of my dreams come true.

May this compilation of poetry expose obscurity and illuminate truth to the reader and may this truth elevate purpose. New journeys are unfolding and new direction has begun. Allow your journey to begin!

POETRY COMPILATION

OPEN EYES

So many things to do in my time;
I've just awakened and found out I've been wasting time.
But you, oh Lord, know all things.
You know my life, you know my dreams.

I am ready to start with you, oh Lord.
Guide me down the path, help me see the way.
It's a place on the other side,
Full of glory, worship, praise, and grace.

Sometimes I am scared and then I remember Holy Spirit is there.
He keeps me in place to see your face.
You've given me love, peace, joy, strength, and hope.
You have given me yourself.

I came a mighty long way to this place I am today,
To go further with you Lord.
I want to see another day, to see another way;
To see all the visions you have given me face to face.

It's because of your love, not my strength.
I shall not be moved. You are mercy and grace.
I shall look back and say,
"That's why I have all this faith."

We're not promised another day, so we need to conquer today.
Not because of my love; it's because of your grace, I am in a new place.
So stop wasting time with all that smoke in your face.
Trust in the Lord and believe because you don't want to find out
you've just awakened out of space.

THROUGH

Guiding me through is all brand new.
Giving my life to you is all I want to do.
I keep focused on you so I can praise and worship you.
See, no one else knows what to do, so if I don't
listen and see, how will I make it through?

I trust and believe there's something brand new, walking with you.
If I make a mistake just get back in line with you
Cause no matter what comes, you'll fight me through.
Only you LORD, knows what to do.

"I'll make a way out of no way," is what the LORD has to say.
Even though this world will say, "Nothing is going your way!"
It doesn't matter what you see; it only matters what I say!
Just keep the faith and always remember, I've
sent my Son; He paid the way.

THROUGH-ALREADY DONE

When the sun shines, it shines through me.
Even when I'm blue, Lord, you still guide me through.

I'm standing strong and I shall not be moved!
Not from the place my Father has me standing.
The Most High is tearing me apart to build me in a new way.
Many fall and stray away.
Oh Lord, on this day you'll say, "I'm just a prayer away."

In the noon day my spirit will say, "Just take
your time. I've already paved the way."
Every time you try to stay, I'll push you in a new way.
"All you have to do is trust in me," is what the Father will say.
So no matter what comes, remember I've made a way.
So rejoice and be glad that our savior paid the
way. Now, we can live in a new way.

BLESSED

I'm blessed no matter what the day might bring.
I'm blessed even when things might seem a mess.
I thank you, Lord, for keeping me from all that stress.

Oh how wonderful and powerful His loving kindness is to me.
I'll trust Him all the days that I shall see.
Oh how good it's going to be!

No matter what comes,
No matter what things might bring,
Just trust in the Lord and you will see
His glory, His peace, and the truth in you and me.
And that truth will set you free for all eternity.

As you can see, I'm blessed. I'm blessed to the extreme.
Have hope and hold on to all your dreams.
See, He wants to bless you and give you your heart's desires.
But you must give up your mess so you can constantly be blessed.

When times seem to get hard and stressed,
Just take the time and remember
How much you're really blessed.

IT'S YOUR CHOICE

It's *my* choice that I love you on today.
No matter what is done, no matter what you might say,
It's righteous, it's pure. It's God way.
The *only* way.

It's not that I fell in love, but it was my choice to love you -
Today and forever.

Accepting love is only from above.
I open my eyes to see within,
To search your heart, to find my way in.
But as you know, it's a choice from within
And you need to let go all of your sin,
so God can come in to fill you up, to deliver you from within.

To take you higher and higher,
He must take you through His holy fire.
Hold on to His mighty grace,
so you can sit before the throne one day and see him face to face.

But remember, it's your choice to choose love, a pure heart.
Right now in this place,
You can choose to be delivered,
and walk in grace.

I RISE

I rise above all things when times get hard.
I rise above the storm and I know how high.
My Lord shows me the path in a very new way.
The path of love he unfolds to me today.

Oh, what a God; what a God he is to me.
Oh, what a mighty God he is to you and me.

Let Him in to guide the way.
He'll lift you up for the world to say.
Glorious God you always know the way.
I'll let you in to show me the way.

No matter what people would say and they will say!
Just understand they only want to know the way.
Only God by Himself knows the way.
Trust in Him on today and understand the way has been made.

WALKING THROUGH THE FIRE

We all have growing pains, but it hurts the most
when we refuse to grow in Christ.
It hinders our walk with our Father.
We must walk through the fire to get to the
other side, so God can have His way.
He wants to take us to a new level of glory and holiness in Him.
God will be exalted in our lives.

We are the light of this world.
Our light must shine and we must smell like Jesus.
So those in the darkness can smell us and walk into His marvelous light.
Their souls will be saved from hell, exchanging it for eternal life.

There's only one way there! You can't buy your
way or manipulate any situation.
You must do it God's way or you won't make it.
The sin will burn in His holy fire and we will
come out white as snow - pure and holy.
You will receive a crown of righteousness.
"Oh the fire it hot and holy."

Some people can't stand to see or examine themselves and their fears.
They are consumed!
Now only if we trust God to bring us out of these painful times of trials.
We need to prepare our hearts, confess our sins.
God will come deliver us from within.

We will continue walking through the fire.
So many things try to get in the way, not wanting us to elevate in Christ
or to walk through the fire that will burn off all the sin anointing us.
So

The choice is yours; you can choose to be scared, stuck, and fall
off; or you can enter hell and let God's holiness take place.
See, we all need to walk through the fire, trusting that our
Father will bring us out, no matter what comes our way.

PATIENT TIMES

When days might seem boring, like nothing is going on,
That's when we have to be patient and endure hard times.

We have to be patient when God says, "Don't move."
Sometimes we try to make things happen
our way, staying busy, trying to
Fix things. And we move right out of line with God.

So when patient times come we need to
meditate, humble ourselves, unwind,
And start taking our time,
Listening to what our Father has to say,
Letting Him always have His way.

We're sitting on the potter's wheel, being made with His wonderful clay.
So, don't be tricked when nothing seems to be happening
or going your way. Just stay patient in your time of faith.
When He releases us to go, everything will flow in a divine way.

So when that particular patient time is over, we will have heard and
Seen what our Father had to say. We will
start to walk with Him His way
A more focused, sensitive and patient way,
Full of God's will and purpose for our lives.

Remember, patient times are always there.
"Be more focused and Aware of a
Patient time."

MERCY & GRACE

I woke one morning with you on my mind,
Thinking about your mercy all the time. I don't deserve your
mercy and grace, but you love me and saved me, anyway.
When I was lost in this world full of mess and stress (I was depressed
and I lost my mind), it was his mercy and grace that saved me.

The Lord could have punished me but He's a merciful God.
Let me tell you about his mercy and grace; it's new every morning.
It endures forever and ever. He doesn't hold
on; He's a God of forgiveness.

Forgiving your past and giving you a new life that's full of hope, love
and prosperity; making you Disciples of Christ, leaders in his army.
Fighting that good fight of faith.
Put on the whole armor of God, marching for victory toward the
mark of the prize and high calling of God in Christ Jesus.

LaDonna Booker-McLemore

WORSHIP YOU

I worship you, Lord.

I worship you.

I worship your Holy name.

We worship you, Lord.

We worship you.

We worship you, Lord.

We worship your Holy name.

I praise and worship you each day, Lord.

You're so awesome in your grace; you're so merciful and precious, Lord.

It was you who saved my soul!

You're so kind and giving in your grace, Lord.

You're so kind and giving in everything you do.

I bow down on my knees, Lord, praying I love you.

GOD IS CALLING ME

God is calling me, God is calling me.

He's calling me to righteousness; he's calling me to new level of glory.

He is delivering me from all mess and stress, pure white as snow.

God is calling me, God is calling me.

He's calling me to excellence; he's calling me for eternity.

He's calling me for the world to see that he's the one dwelling in me.

Can't you hear the calling of the bells ringing for your soul?

You shall rise to the calling of the Most High.

He's calling me to set you free,

So you can see that he's the one dwelling in me for eternity.

So if God is calling you, don't be ashamed; let him have his way.

He will break you and make you into his disciples.

See, the world needs our gifts, our fruit.

It helps loose them, directing them to Christ.

I'LL TRUST HIM

I'll trust him all my days to be, I'll trust you in every way.
He has shown me that He's faithful, full of joy and peace,
With a heart so big for you and me. It's big enough for
the whole world to see that he dwells in me.

He's always there, listening and holding me tight, helping
me see he has so much in store for me to receive.
Rewarding me with eternity.
I'll trust him all my days to see.
I'll trust him in every way.

"Oh, how I love you."

I just want to stay in your presence.
It's full of joy and peace so sweet and good to me.
No matter what I do, you're still the same.

"Full of love"

You say, "Repent; don't be ashamed." I trust in you; I shall remain.
For faith is the substance of things not seen!
I'll trust you to bring what's not seen to my vision.

Like you said, your word shall not come back
to you void without accomplishing.
I'll trust you for eternity.

WHAT MUST I SAY?

What must I say, what must I say?
We must keep our eyes on the Most High at all times.
It's very important to listen to our Father,
But it's a choice, because once we walk out of His
will and grace, we will fall, hitting our face.

Hey, what must I say?
If we're trying to do it our way, it going to waste away!
All the way.
"What are we, crazy men?"

Wait a minute, wait a minute.
His word says be sober at all times, casting all our cares upon
Him; standing strong in our faith, humble before our Father.
When we have gotten out of line, He's a merciful
God, still making a way when we've lost ours;
With open arms, unconditional love that the world can't give us.

I'm sorry that you had to hit your face.
Next time stay in His will and grace.
Keep your mind on things above.
So you won't get pushed and shoved by the
devil that has no power anyway,
Unless you make room for him to stay, to
torment, destroying your will, your way.

Don't be a fool on today!
Kick him out and he'll flee.
We have the power, Jesus is always telling me.
We have the victory for eternity.
"Hey, what must I say?"

I guess you learned your lesson for the day.
So study and stay in your word every day.
You'll be cleansed for Him to have His way; having on
your armor to press forward to win and conquer.

Not just today but every night and day, in every way.

IN SEARCH

I searched and searched but couldn't find one
who could love me the way you do.
I did the drugs, I didn't find you there.
I sold my body! I still didn't find you.
I also let that man misuse me for years.
All hell broke loose. I still didn't find you.
"See, I was lost. I didn't even know I was in search of you, Lord."

It wasn't until I fell down on my knees and called your name, Jesus,
That I received your love, life, hope, and dreams.
Needed relationship, someone to talk to when no
one else understands - not even myself.

That's why I have to press, remembering that I only
found love in you when times get hard.
I must yield myself to the spirit of God that dwells down in me.
You see, He knows what I need right at that moment, or I can choose
to take off my robe of righteousness and let my flesh have its way.
The situation will be there after I'm done, so I will just press and
humble myself and let die whatever needs to die, letting God's
spirit arise to handle the situation that I can't fix anyway.

So I thank you, Lord, for the life that dwells down in me. I thank you
Jesus for resurrecting me, for the healing in my mind, for setting me free.
I'll keep my eyes on you and try not to analyze what I
don't understand anymore, letting Holy Spirit flow.

I will go in faith, coming out victoriously, knowing it's not about me.
But when you exalt me, taking me higher and higher, your glory will be
revealed in my life and I will always sing praises in your son Jesus' name.

LOVE BETWEEN US

Oh, how wonderful your love is to me.
They don't understand until they wait and see how
longsuffering this charity is for you unto me.
You're so kind and giving on our behalf for us to have your love.

We're trusting each other to endure all things.
Love is full of loyalty that one must see and be,
God's love, not jealousy.
We will keep him in our hearts for eternity so we
can always see the truth in you and me.
We'll be free and in peace. Oh, how good it is to me.
This love is full of joy and prosperity.
Defending one another so sin can't come in, so when times are
hard and stressed, we'll remember faith, hope and love!
Oh how it conquers all things till the end.
We are blessed!

OUR GOD IS WORTHY

In the midst of the storm, our God is worthy.

He's never left my side; our God is worthy.

He's been a comforter in my time of need. He is a God of understanding, a God of peace. He's worthy of all praise.

Sometimes in life we go through things and most situations are so discouraging.

I had to learn to let God guide me through for I know He knows what's best for me to do.

I had to take my eyes off the situation.

I had to learn how to pay close attention to what the Lord was saying to my heart.

When I thought He left me, He was there from the start.

He's worthy. Yea, He's worthy of all the praise.

IN YOUR PRESENCE

In your presence is where I want to be.

In your presence I humble myself to thee.

My Holy Father,

I submit to your spirit; He takes me there.

In your presence, that's where I want to be, as you
touch me with your holy power to do your will, helping
me to see the road you have set before me.

In your presence I get whatever I might need: patience, joy,
peace, healing - as you direct me to a new level in you.

In your presence is where I want to be.

"It's so calm."

In your presence I praise and worship thee, receiving
messages, getting visions, as I tap into your power,
tearing down strongholds in my life and mind.

Only in the spiritual realm can a child of God flow. In
your presence, that's where we all need to be.

MY FIRST TRUE LOVE

You're my first and true love from heaven above.

I sing praise to your name;

Lord you know you reign.

You're my first and true love from heaven above.

My first and true love,

Holy and faithful to me.

You cleansed my soul.

I lift my hands to thee.

What an awesome God who gave me a new life.

He's an unconditional God. What more can I say?

You're my first and true love from heaven above.

I sing praise to your name; Lord you reign.

SPIRITUAL ATTACK

I am not wasting my time writing these rhymes,
Knowing who I am, being sober at times. Fighting
spiritual crimes, getting what's mine.

Rejoicing and praying for souls. He's the only one I flow for.
Twenty-four seven, I will make it to heaven.
Standing in the gap, can't get a nap, not wanting them to
snap; praying and pressing, they're being attacked.
So now you know why I must flow: this spiritual attack.

All demons step back.
Watch out! You might get a holy smack!
Now it goes to show who the one in control is.

He's the Lord who knows all things, wakes me
up in my dreams, stopping the screams.
Praising His name, knowing I have holy game in the spiritual realm.
See His marvelous light shining in the dim.
Our unsaved friends need to check themselves before
this world wrecks them and takes them out.

You don't have to sell out to hell, receiving eternal jail.
Choose life and light, not stress - being depressed.
See, you will get beat in these streets for sure.

I'm free, free indeed to do His will.
So pick life and fight that good fight of faith so you can attack.
Your enemies will step back!

LISTEN & SEE

I've been through so many things in my time.

I couldn't understand until things started to unwind.

All I had to do is keep my eyes on you but now I know
I have to press my way through and trust, knowing
that you're with me, seeing me all the way.

I had to have faith and get in line with you, praying and listening.

Now I see what you've been trying to show me:

"The big picture"

Of your will for my life.

Sometimes Father, you allow us to turn the wrong way.

To get stuck in the mud.

It's a good place. We cry for help.

You pull us out of our mess, clean our face, so we can see we need
to keep our eyes on you at all times; so we can know what to do.

When you say move; when you say stop; when you say give; when
you say speak; I will be humble and ready to do as you say.

LIFE OR DEATH

You can have all your heart desires,

but if you don't have Christ you don't have anything.

See, I know who I am without materialistic things:

A child of the Most High God and I know my dreams.

Sometimes people make me want to scream.

It's only about their clothes, cars and how much
bling; they only have pipe dreams.

People don't even want to step on my scene.

Eternal life!

They don't want to fight.

See, they laugh at my music, at how I praise your holy name.

My God, that's a shame; they don't even know you rule
and reign. The devil has their life, playing a game.

Sex, money, drugs, living in the fast lane;
all he has to offer is eternal hell!

I'm praying that God will remove the veil from their eyes so they can
see that the Bible isn't a lie. Jesus really did die for you and me.

Give Him a chance, you'll see hell isn't the place for you or me, but
soon this world will come to an end; Satan and his angels didn't win.

The Most High cast them out to the pits of hell, so if you choose not to trust in Him, you'll have your part, too, in the lake of fire!

Don't get caught up in this world if you want to make it to heaven. 1-2-3-4-5-6, it was completed; seven, he rested. We have to do our part, so don't get caught up in this mess.

Saving souls, that's what it's all about - not trying to impress, wearing your ice, idolizing death and famous stars.

I pray that my light will make you free because
God didn't create us for all this nonsense.

He made us for praise and worship.

But it's your choice what you will receive: life or death!

Plain and simple, we'll all be judged in the end by our Lord and savior.

Just drop this note trying to save you.

TESTIMONY

Girl, don't you know you're worthy?

Our body's a living sacrifice, so stop trying to entice and get a righteous life. I'm here trying to save your souls from eternal hell.

Receive eternal life – that's the way to go; get off the drugs and corners and follow me, having goals.

Wait a minute, wait a minute. Don't think I don't know I come from the hood, where drinking and partying is all good.

That kind of life is not the way to be.

I used to dance and get high; the enemy was destroying me. I was praying for my life, not knowing who I was - dying inside; feeling stressed, depressed, not even wanting to get dressed.

I needed something new; I was chasing after a man who didn't even want to hold my hand.

You see, my mind was really messed up. That's why Jesus died for me, redeeming my life, giving me a new chance to do a new dance -holy as can be. No man can undress me with his eyes; he will see Holy Spirit is the one that dwells in me.

Girl, don't look back; it was not all that. So press and press until you have won, and you'll be complete in Christ.

I AM COMING OUT

I am coming out.

I want the world to know God is in control.

Let me tell somebody that He's been so good to me. He renewed my mind and set me free. He's tearing down the strongholds in my life and mind. It feels so good, so good to me. He set me free.

He shut the door on all hell from tormenting me.

My mind, my thoughts are of good courage and full of peace.

Hey, what must I say? Our God is good full of mercy and grace.

I'm coming out. I want the world to know God is the only one in control of my life.

In Him we live, in Him we move, and have our being.

We lift our hands, we praise His name, and do our dance.

You rule and reign, Lord. What must I say?

See, I'm coming out and His glory is going to show; nobody can stop this flow.

LaDonna Booker-McLemore

NEW BEGINNINGS

In life you can always start over,
If you don't like the way things are going.
The things we do set our destiny;
Never let adversities get the best of you.
Stand strong; the past is gone.

A new beginning!
The Lord is setting me free; He's directing my steps as I apply His word.
He's always speaking boldly into my life.

Natural man can't understand
It's His holy plan.
So I'm pressing toward my vision,
Making good decisions, using intuition in all situations.

Never chase after worldly things.
Store my treasures in heavenly dreams.
I want to see the king who knows all things;
righteousness gleams like bling.

Lost souls will transform into pure gold.
This world is so ugly and cold, so choose the right road.

We're living in perilous days!

Eternal life is a new beginning.
The choice is yours.
Little girls and boys are having troubled minds.
They're lost in a world of crime.
So let your life shine.

Lord, captivate their broken hearts with your undying love.
Let them know that Jesus is a new start.
AMEN

LaDonna Booker-McLemore

I WILL STAND

If it doesn't work the first time, don't give up.
Just keep on trying and you'll succeed.
You will conquer everything if you keep on keeping on.
We have to command the mountains to move out
of our way; in Jesus' name it will be done.
**See, it's only hard if that's the way you think;
we have the power if we have the faith!**

Sometimes we have to command our flesh to obey our spirit man, and
God is not a man that he can lie; so know that your environment will lie.
Whose report will you believe?

Now there's a time and a season for everything,
so know what season you're in.
In order to receive new things you must do different things.
Do what is right and truthful and not what man thinks is
correct, because obedience is better than sacrifice.
Never forget the vision God gave you, always praising His holy name.
Love your enemies when times are good, never telling them I told you so!
Stay humble and you'll always win.
Bless your enemies in Jesus' name.
You tell me, Lord, to identify individuals by whether
they're being good or bad, because what's in a man's
heart will come out his mouth eventually.

"Obey you if I love you" is what the Most High says.
Make sure your foundation is built upon your word and not
man's because when the winds of life blow, you'll be able to
stand firmly, knowing it's not about me; it's about my Father.

THE VOID

Sometimes it's hard for me to express how I'm felling, the feeling of
having something missing deep within - a void where God is not present.

I understand that for most of my life I was
filling that void with several things:
Drinking, drugs, sex, etc.
Now I'm praying, asking God to enter that
place that's very dry and lonely.
I remember feeling like nobody loved me,
wanting someone to hold me at night.

Only God can embrace, taking away all the pain that has built
up over the years from family, men, and so-called friends.
Only God knows what I really need, even when I don't know.

So on today, I allow the Most High into all the dry areas
of life, so light and love can fill the VOID of life.

ACCEPTING LOVE

When I look at you I see a strong woman of God who
treads upon lions and cobras to conquer her dreams.

You are a woman with a heart full of acceptance and
unconditional love that flows from the depths of her
being as she connects with the holy King.

Her name is Accepting Love.

She accepts the will of God that's full of truth
that makes her whole in Christ.

This is what the Lord thinks of me, so there is nothing to say;
I will just be me because he loves me unconditionally,

In spite of the things I've done.

I'm so overwhelmed by his perfect love that
no man or situation can take away.

So on today, I will count it all joy that my Father gave me
a name that's part of His will as the Lady of Truth who
has accepted His word and walks in truth. So be it.

FAITHFUL WALK

When I can't see it, I will still believe it.
Father, that's what it's all about: hope (*divine*
hope), faith, love, and dreams.
When I never had anything, no one showed me how to
accomplish in life. "But God," who knows all things, says take
this faithful walk with me down a road you've never been on
before, where blessings, love, prosperity, and peace abide.

You need to believe in me and yourself at all times, that I
will be by your side every step of the way, teaching, showing
you my perspective of things. It's a totally new way.
So come and take this faithful walk down a
road you've never been on before.

I shall bring it to pass, full of mercy and grace.

I'll take care of the rest if you move out of my way.
Just keep doing as I told you and
"Fret not; it only causes harm," hindering your walk.

I've given you power, love, and a sound mind to conquer all
that fear, so tap in and plug into my power, my dear child.
Continue walking that road of faith.
I'm directing your path and you shall not stumble,
or fall, or stray in the opposite way.
Press and press toward the prize and you shall
win that faithful walk of faith.

LaDonna Booker-McLemore

VIRTUOUS VESSEL

Who is this Virtuous woman of God? "Administrating Development!"
She's administering to the saints, developing our gifts and talents,
making us Disciples of Christ, sending Pure Hope into the world
flying on eagle's wings, full of God's will, fishing for souls.

Who is this virtuous woman of God? She's
Administrating Development, full of love flowing from
the depths of her soul - God's special vessel.
See, His glory is so cloudy in her life that everywhere
she goes people don't know why, but there's something
special about that lady. That's what they say.
We are drawn in by the love of God in this
anointed virtuous woman's life.

My Father has chosen this woman to be over our lives.
Oh, how special that makes me feel that He has
chosen me to be part of this vision.
I really know my Father is directing me and using this virtuous
woman to administrate in my life his will, to develop every talent,
gift, and purpose into what God has called me to be in this world.

She has been such a positive influence in my life: a righteous, holy,
faithful, and a beautiful example of what a virtuous woman of God is.
Her boldness is outstanding in my point of
view, just the way he made her.
She's isn't ashamed of being a powerful woman.
When I see her I don't see gender; I see an obedient vessel
God's spirit dwells in, one that's willing and ready.

I AM PRESSING

I want sit back, being pressed against the wall, praising
the Most High's name, and I won't be ashamed.
I'm standing tall knowing who rules and reigns in my life.
Now, I'm stepping out with the gifts that he gave me, making
an attack, all my enemies step back because the greater one
that's within helps me to stand to do His perfect will.

I'm forgetting all the things behind me, pressing
toward the mark of the prize.
I thank the Lord that I finally realized a renewed
mind is what he gave me, saved me with the blood
of the lamb as I press toward all my dreams.

LaDonna Booker-McLemore

PERILOUS TIMES

I just want to inform those who don't understand
that we're living in perilous times.

Spiritual warfare is taking place in the mind, the battlefield.

This world is coming to an end.

We're going to be judged in the end for all our sins.

So if you want to see his face, you need to start running this spiritual
race. Time out for games; doesn't be ashamed to call his Holy name.

The Lord rules and reigns, and He's the only one who
can make your life change, so open your eyes to see that
we're living in the last days – perilous times.

Children are killing each other, not respecting their mothers, selling
drugs, sleeping with scrubs, thugs, thinking it's life, losing their
minds, taking what's yours but I'm fighting for what's mine.

So many voids in this world and people fill them with so many
things (only God's love, not materialistic things). They're not even
fighting for their hopes and dreams; dying of an eternal death.

Look, I'm not trying to hate; I just want to elevate. Boldness, that's what this generation needs to feel some conviction, falling down on their hands and knees, saying, Jesus please.

It's time to wake up and receive salvation, become part of this holy nation, exchanging that old life, letting him have his way to mold you as you sit on the potter's wheel; now that's the real.

God's love is more than enough; it surpasses all things. Hallelujah! Have faith and come and step on my scene.

You're not whack; you're becoming a royal priest, so lift your hands and sing. We're living in perilous day.

See, what many people don't understand is that everything in this world fades away.

All the money, power, will be devoured by the supreme ruler of our hearts and soul, because there's only two ways to go: heaven or hell. Which will you decide?

SPIRITUAL RACE

You set my heart on fire, setting me in search of your power.
Your spirit is taking me higher and higher into your spiritual realm.
I tap and plug into your power; you know what I'm saying.

I want to see that man loosed on the corner, breaking the
devil's stronghold and power in his life and mind.
Can't you see what I'm doing? My Father's business.
He sent me to be Accepting Love.

See, no matter what comes, I won't run, but facing my fears,
stepping out, my dear, with God's anointing on my tongue,
cutting those demonic spirits in half with my two-edged sword.
Never giving the enemy power over my life, but letting Holy
Spirit, bad as he wanna be, arise in these perilous days.

We are called to be, so open your eyes and see that
Jesus didn't play; he died for you and me.
Read it in John three, verses sixteen and seventeen.
Now get ready; get ready with your armor of God and stop
playing but getting in place to win this spiritual race.

Ephesians six, verses eleven through nineteen.
This isn't about flesh and blood but about principalities with spiritual
eyes to see that we're fighting against power, against the rulers of the
darkness of this world, against spiritual wickedness in high places.

So take your face out of space; trust in his will and grace.
Let God's spirit arise in these evil days, having your
loins girt with your belt of truth, your shoes of peace
so you can step out, speaking the gospel.

Now, no matter what comes, taking my shield
of faith, can't even see your face.
Jesus died in your place.
Receive your salvation; we're part of a holy nation,
running, winning victory for eternity.

WHATSOEVER

Hold on when you're not feeling strong.
Hold on and never allow yourself to go to
depression's places in your mind.
Rejoice in the Lord and think on these things.

Think on things that are true; it's true that life is rough. However, I will
seek my heavenly Father's face, keeping my eyes on the mark of the prize.

Whatsoever things are just, the promises of God in His
word are honorable if you are in covenant with him.

Whatsoever things are pure, Jesus is pure - a sinless man who died
for our sins so we can enter our Father's presence any time.

Think on things that are lovely.
God is love and unconditional to us all the time.

Think on things that are of a good report and if there
is any virtue or anything praiseworthy, think on these
things and you'll be filled with joy and peace.

HE IS THE GREAT I AM

I am more than a conqueror and can do all things because
the Holy King said so. Therefore, it shall be done.

I am a royal priest, joint heirs with Christ, and he's the one
living his righteousness through me, so I'm righteous.

I am a child of the Most High God and his Spirit teaches
me His way, comforting me all the away to eternity

I have faith, hope, and love; the greatest of them is love; therefore, I
will fear no man, walking in power, having a sound mind at all times.

We shall do greater works in the name of Jesus.

It's the Most High's will.

When I'm weak he shows up strong, and it encourages me to
hold on because in him we live, move, and have our being.

See, this walk is not about us; it's about the Holy King.

He's the great I AM.

I RELEASE THE PAIN

I remember when I was little, watching mom go through
so many things, trying to feed four kids with little
money, eating neck bones with green beans.
She tried to stay strong; adversities had her mind so gone.
She was full of anger with pain, smoking weed to stay
sane, drinking day after day to numb the pain.
She didn't know how to regain her soul; it was
dying and we felt her rage each day.

I understood; I withstood with unconditional love,
holding her in my arms with a soft rub.
She was a good person. It was hard to see at times,
asking me to get her a dime; it was a crime.
Our house was the spot on the block.
People in and out late at night; I grew up full
of fright with no respect for self.
See, my role model was a crack fiend that lost her dreams.
Her soul was in anguish as she screamed while getting
beat, as I watched nightmares in my sleep.

My childhood was stolen by poverty, abuse, drugs and no love.
I only wanted someone to show me love.
My mom did the best she could; I forgive her only if she could.
I grew up chasing after men and in the end I was living in sin;
now I'm taking the pen, helping someone get delivered within.

Jesus is the light, the one who comes to give us light more abundantly.
So release your burdens and pain so you can gain and
feel his love - unconditional love, no more shame.
I release it all, I release it all. I release the pain.

ATONING WASH

He's cleansing the walls that no man can clean; only by
his atoning spirit, washing with the blood of the lamb,
sparkling like gold, coming out whole - victoriously.

God is cleaning the walls of my soul, piece by piece,
continuing the good He started in me.

God is manifesting the things that I saw in the spirit.

You have to suffer, having faith to walk this walk, always pressing,
knowing that no weapon formed against you shall prosper.

The battle has already been won.

He's God almighty, He's everything. He is king of kings and lord
of lords; no man can shut the door that God has opened.

He's helping me place things in order so His perfect plan can come forth.

I praise my Father, knowing he rules and reigns over everything
as he cleanses the walls that no man can clean.

LaDonna Booker-McLemore

THERE ARE TIMES

There are times when life is full of pain and the rain seems
to never stop; wanting to give up, ending it all.

Then I remember faith and hope; they carried
me through to another day.

There are times when frustration and fear try to draw
near. I have to hear the silent voice and resist the noise,
knowing that my creator loves me unconditionally.

See, it a choice and we choose our state of mind by the
things we meditate on, whether being good or bad.

One will make you happy, the other will make you sad.

Choose 'good' because bad will have you stressing,
never dressing, pressing toward depression.

Laughter is medicine to the heart and soul; it's
better than a man and even gold.

For the joy of the Lord is my strength, strengthening us to
overcome any adversities, situations or obstacles that may arise.

It will arise; I will over ride.

I'm like the lion of the Tribe of Judah, taking dominion
over it all, never letting strife in my life.

It cuts like a knife tearing down, tearing down relationships!
There are so many things and so many times;
just unwind and live life to the fullest.

EVERYTHING

Love is all I need. You see, if you have love you
have everything because God is love.

I have everything my heart desires and it sets my soul on
fire, chasing after that unconditional love that endures
forever even in the midst of our adversities.

I have everything under the sun. "I have love."

One day a little seed was planted in my heart and that love has brought
me out of the dark, blossoming into a beautiful flower; watering my
spirit, mind, and soul with rushing love that no man can take away.

I finally have everything and it's like an awesome dream I live every day.

When this world comes to an end everything will vanish,
but faith, hope, and love will endure forever.

Love is unconditional when your mate seems to hate.

Love is very patient when your children disobey, and when things are not going our way, love doesn't demand its own way.

Love is kind to our worse enemies.

Love doesn't put itself on high; only God can exalt when one is humble.

Love is always forgiving one's evil sins; it's not rude or selfish.

Love is a helping hand when one is in need.

Love believes in others' dreams; love is loyal to friendship and devoted to what matters.

God is love!

BEAUTIFUL

When I look at you, I see beauty flowing from the
depths of your soul like a clear blue stream.

The glory of God is a radiant light shining into very dark places.

I see you bowed down in his presence, seeking
his face, loving everything that's holy.

I see you in the spirit being very still, not making a
move until Father God reveals his next steps.

You are an obedient vessel of GOD, going to glorious places. Beauty
is her name and God is beautiful in this virtuous vessel, leading
God's sheep to the most holy of holiest places in the spirit.

Beauty meditates on his word every day, staying
cleansed and washed in the blood of the lamb.

A spiritual mother - that's what she is to me; someone I can
talk to, learning how to walk in the brand new life.

If you want to see what God can do, look at this beautiful woman,
Bishop Mariea Claxton, and be amazed by the power of God.

IN THE MIDST OF THE STORM

In the midst of the storm you have to know that God is worthy.
He will never leave our side; He's worthy!

He's a present help in our time of need; he's been a God of
understanding, a God of peace. He's worthy, worthy of all our praise.

Most times in life we go through things and most
situations can seem so discouraging.
We have to have to faith, putting our trust in God,
knowing that He is more than able.

Give the Most High praise throughout the day and be
not dismayed 'cause he's worthy of all our praises.

See, in the midst of the storm our God is worthy;
I'm never ashamed to praise his name.
The Lord rules and reigns above all things.

He's a holy king that never leaves or forsakes; he's going to
take us and transform us into the image of Christ.

So just hold on, having faith, and don't live
by sight in the midst of the storm.

SPIRITUAL WARFARE

I'm having my loins girded with my belt of truth, coming
against the kingdom of darkness with my spirit man.

See, I'm not going to sit back, being pressed against the wall.

The Lord is delivering me, now I'm standing tall, making my
enemies look small, representing the kingdom of God.

Saving souls from eternal hell bringing the Shekinah
light of glory in very dark places.

Sweet smelling aroma is going up in praise,
worshipping in spirit and truth.

I'm making an attack and all my enemies are stepping back,
knowing the power and authority within; Jesus is my best friend.

I've been anointed to face my fear; I'm no longer
believing a lie; the deceiver has been exposed.

Staying sober at all times, fighting spiritual crimes, letting the
joy of the Lord be my strength living in the last days,

Doing my father's will, shedding light, setting minds free,
elevating the youth to see that Jesus can set them free from
this dying world, making them whole and complete.

Their souls will be purified, made pure as gold, so hold on to
the truth and praise your way to His everlasting will.

We're in a spiritual war; the battle field is the
mind, so store your treasures in heaven.

Keep your mind on things above, casting down anything that's not of
God, and your mind will be renewed against the darkness and lies.

I CRY WITH MY WHOLE HEART

I cry with my whole heart; hear me, oh Lord.

I cry with my whole heart, tears of joy.

I will keep your statutes, praising and
worshipping you, because I want to.

See, I cried unto the Lord and he saved me;
therefore, I will obey His will.

I cry in his presence - connecting, feeling his unconditional love
that no man can give; releasing unto him all my worries and cares,
knowing he will carry me through the raging storms of life.

Jesus Christ paid the way, so I cry with my whole heart that
he delivered me from the dark into his glorious light.

I cry with my whole heart for the ones lost and can't
see; Holy Spirit helps me to pray for thee.

I cry with my whole heart, never ashamed,
giving him my burdens and pain.

The clouds, the rain - he's above it all,

So I cry with my whole heart, his endless love.

I AM A NEW CREATION IN CHRIST

As I reminisce on the things I used to indulge in (sex,
lust, and immorality lead me to a place of salvation), now
I'm part of a holy nation, joint heir with Christ.

Now looking at my life, there's no more enticement;
I'm a new creation, not chasing after a man but chasing
after the only man who died for my sins.

You see, he loves me unconditionally, never rejecting
me, but loving me with his Holy Spirit.

I'm going from glory to glory, not trying to be in a hurry but
letting him purge me, deliver me, set me free for all eternity.

See, he's judging me with his holy word and most think they
will get away with it, but in the end we will sit before the
mighty king who brings all hopes and dreams to pass.

So open your eyes and see that accepting Christ is
the way to wisdom - not rejecting him.

He'll give you joy within, taking away all the sin; continue
that good work until the day of Christ's coming.

I just accept his love; we don't have to push or shove,
just lifting our hands, praising his name, confessing
our sins so we can enter his presence.

As I open my eyes to spiritual things, my heart sings
because he can do the impossible things, with ears
to hear, steering me all the way to eternity.

Now no man can be against me if Christ is for me, and all
the doors are open for me; just watch and see. Your eyes
will be filled with amazement at the power of God.

The Most High has anointed me and I'm
flowing His word in a unique way.

I know it's not me but it's he who dwells on the inside, who gives
you a new life if you're willing to exchange that old one.

LISTEN UP

He comes like a thief in the night dressed in sheep
clothes, deceiving the mind with gentle words.

He comes to devour your heart and soul, draining you till you fall apart.

It's real old; he's a trick. He might be tall,
dark, and handsome but he's slick.

Listen up, listen up.

We have to put on the whole armor of God.

To the world it's odd.

Now be careful what you listen to.

The videos you watch might seem top notch but it's full of lust; it's dark.

Think not twice but resist it as soon as it comes.

Never give the flesh what it wants; don't be dumb!

Overcome; tap into the power of his word and
make it manifest. Receive the best:

His will!

WORTHY PRAISE

Praise His name, praise His name, for God is
worthy. Come on and praise His name.

God is worthy, come on and praise His name.

Lift up the Most High and praise his name.

God is worthy, come on and praise his name.

God is mighty before all things, even our problems. If we just keep
our eyes on Him we'll see that He's worthy of praise and worship.

See, if we obey we will see his glory, and his
righteousness is committed to loving us.

I will lift up your name high as the heavens because
you rule and reign above all things.

I lift Him up and praise His name, knowing he's worthy of praise.

I'm never ashamed to give my Father the highest praise.

So come on and praise his name, praise his name!

YOUR WILL BE DONE

Your will be done, your will be done. It will be done in my life! I shall not move around from place to place because I'm doing your will.

I shall stand steadfast in the faith doing your will.

Your will be done, your will be done like you said in your word.

See, you're not a man that you shall lie; like you
said in your word, your will be done.

I will wait, stand, and see your word manifest in my
life and your glory will be revealed in my life.

It's because of my will but your will be done, like you said in your word!

I'm steeping out in the faith, walking; and my steps won't be strained.

When I run I shall not stumble or fall.

My steps are ordered by the Lord.

I will always humble myself and your will be
done like you said in your word.

Your will be done like it is in heaven and earth.

JESUS

Jesus, Jesus, Jesus; there's power in that name.

You rule, you reign, always remaining the same; full of
mercy and grace - unconditional love for us all.

See, He came to walk that holy walk, to talk that gospel talk, to die for
our sins, our family and friends that couldn't save us or even pray for us.

But on Calvary, Jesus gave His precious life for you and me.

They stretched Him out, hung Him on the cross.

They pierced him in his side.

He died so that we could arise, setting us free for all eternity.

He's the living bread that I feed on and the resurrection of my life.

You have the choice now to receive eternity; it's an
opportunity to reunite with our Holy Father.

You might call Him Jehovah; I call Him my sweet, precious Daddy.

So don't be ashamed on today to call his holy name.

He came to die in your name and that wasn't a game.

Jesus, Jesus, Jesus; oh how I love that name, Jesus.

Jesus, Jesus, Jesus; there's power in that name.

LaDonna Booker-McLemore

HOLDING IT DOWN

See, we have to hold it down.

We don't even have time to play around with sin!

We must hold it down for the kingdom of heaven.

See, I'm stepping on the scene, praising my king, making a
noise, a joyful noise for the only man that died for my sins.

So many things come in the midst of the day, trying to
make me fall off and stray away but I lift my hands, praising
my king for eternal things, my hope and dreams.

Now I'm standing on His word; the roots go deep within, so as
the rivers flow and the winds blow, I want be swept off my feet.

I keep my eyes on him; he keeps me in perfect peace.

I'm a true Disciple of Christ, a soldier in His army
- pressing toward the mark of the prize.

You better open your eyes and realize that we're living in the last
days, the last stage, so many people lost, trying to get paid!

So you better store your treasures in eternal things because in the end
only the ones that are holding it down for Christ will be standing.

THE LORD OF THE BREAKTHROUGH

See, my father's love is like the morning dew, guiding me through.

I'm here to guide you to the Lord of the breakthrough.

See He knew before Matthew and even before Jews that the way you're living life is overdue, so now is the time to follow through.

Life with Christ is sweet like honeydew, so release your burdens like a corkscrew and enter the newness of life.

Now overcome because we're not dumb; the Lord is the only one who can make our enemies run like a gun!

It was said and done when Jesus died on the cross.

The enemy will treat you like a hit and run!

So don't be stunned; read your Bible; it tells you we've already won.

This new life has just begun, so accept it - all or none. Because He was whipped, now we have fellowship, partnership; no need for an ego trip.

We now have friendship, we're close-knit.
He's preparing me for courtship.

See, He's the Lord of the breakthrough guiding
me through to everything that's new.

LADY

I had to get rid of all my old clothes because I'm a lady now.

I'm dressing with self-respect, earning my check with dignity, not sitting around letting a man misuse me sexually because he takes care of me!

I have to love me for me.

I'm getting myself together, focusing on God,
and can't any man approach me without

R-E-S-P-E-C-T

I'm taking back everything that was stolen: my
mind, my soul, my heart and body.

I no longer have time for old things.

I must stimulate my mind, spirit and soul as I press away from the old.

I'm being ushered to my new life and God
is making me a wife for Christ.

So, thanks to my Father God for sending His precious son, Jesus Christ.

I am a lady now.

TRUTH

My heart and soul are full of so many talents and dreams.

Tears stream from my eyes as I look at the past.

I now know that I have to grasp the time of my season,
understanding everything happens for a reason.

I now look through the eyes of faith, escaping
the past so I can reach my dreams.

Beautiful Black Woman, coming to the scene.

I'm giving birth one at a time.

It's time for me to finally shine and can't any man stop my destiny.

See, I put the enemy within to death.

I'm pressing toward my vision, making good decisions in all situations, getting revelations, never hating mankind knowing I'm unique.

I've soul searched and made it out of the wilderness, giving back to society to make a stand for something or you're nothing but stressed out, full of mess, not seeing the truth that you're older with the mind of a youth.

The truth will set us free to see that the future has something valuable to offer if were willing to do what's necessary.

Never procrastinate! Elevate your mind, watch negative people; they're full of hate.

Now sit back and unwind; prosperity will shine like bling.

You will see all your dreams in the end.

SO MANY DREAMS

Martin Luther King had so many dreams that
became a reality for you and me.

So why are we taking it for granted as we fill
our minds with dysfunctional things?

Martin Luther King had big dreams that had
a profound effect on mankind.

So where are *our* dreams?

Do you have any dreams?

See, he took a stand for righteousness, so will you?

Martin Luther King had so many dreams that
blacks and whites would love one another.

So look at what you are doing. Are you getting along now that he's gone?

Mr. King fought for so many things; it was for you and me - Black unity!

You be happy and celebrate Dr. Martin Luther
King, Jr.'s birthday by having big dreams.

By LaTelle & Mom

LaDonna Booker-McLemore

THE CHOICE IS YOURS

I can lead you to the water but I can't make you drink
and when I'm gone it's going to make you think.
The choice is yours, but "either or," we're going
to be judged before the holy king.
See, I'm walking in truth, elevating the youth, spreading
the word in a way that's going to be heard.
It's out of the norm, no time for lukewarm; you need to be
reborn, and imitating Christ is part of your new your life.

Now you need to conquer your dreams; step on the scene.
I know you want the bling, so look to the holy king who
knows all things. He'll make your spirit sing.
In the midnight hour God will give you power so make
a stand, be a man. I know you can; your man ran.

Now he's on the streets, getting beat, looking for heat, reaping it all.
He's running for his life; you better call his holy
name. You're living insane for the fame.
You're going to feel the pain in your life!

You stabbed yourself in the back with your own knife; look at your life.

Now you're on the ground; God will bring you around, redeeming your
dreams, making your enemies scream. But the choice is yours; "either
or," we're going to be judged before the holy king who knows all things.

So once again I can lead you to the water but I can't make you drink,
and when I'm gone, what I told you is going to make you think.
The choice is yours; "either or," we're going
to be judged before the holy king.

HAVE HOPE

Poverty, violence, drug abuse and sex; seeing your mother getting
beat, father going to jail, not knowing what's coming next.
Selling drugs, stealing cars, taking another man's
life; now that's what the street life is like!

That kind of life is full of darkness and pain; can't stop the rain and
not even being ashamed that you got caught up living insane.
That's why I'm flowing these lyrics to help you change your mind,
So that you don't have to live a dysfunctional life, fighting crime.

Think back on when you were little, full of so many dreams;
did you like to write, dance or sing? Or even play ball?
If so, just know that there's something deep on
the inside that needs to come alive!

So tap into that inner strength and let that old
man go! A new one will enter in.
All you have to do is look at yourself the way God does
and press toward the vision with faith and works.

It might not be easy in the beginning and I understand if you
scream, but you must remain patient when situations arise; know
that they come to test you, building you strong; you'll carry on.

The dark clouds will pass on and the sunlight
will shine; we're part of the vine.
Now know that's its divine and you'll be living fine.
Trust in your Father God and in the gifts and talents he gave you.
You will make it through victoriously,
So have hope.

PURE HOPE

When you're pure, you better believe the individual is sure
to stand, standing on a solid foundation with character.
When one is pure he's spotless, like a beautiful diamond gleaming with
light; we have been brought with a price by the blood of the lamb.

Hope - when you hope, you're expecting, never neglecting the desires
that set your soul on fire, trusting in the Lord; the enemy is a liar.
When you hope, you cherish it with anticipation until it's fulfilled,
knowing it's the Lord's will, standing still, and He'll reveal what's real.

Though the vision tarries, never get weary; and in the end you'll succeed.
We're blessed, indeed, always interceding - sowing beautiful seeds.
You'll reap a harvest in time of need.

Pure Hope is God's will!
He has given us a vision, provision; we have to make the right
decisions, standing in one accord, using our two-edged sword.
God has ordained Pure Hope, sustained us and
corrected us; and we have no weakness in Christ.
He has strengthened us to overcome with faith.
We have escaped from that same old place and I'm
thanking God for His mercy and grace.

So I thank Pure Hope; it gave me a dream.
I now know who I am; my spirit sings Hallelujah!

Pure Hope is not a joke; we're a Renewed Covenant
Church! Bearing fruit - good fruit of all kinds, praising
God, fighting spiritual crimes; we're one of a kind.
I know the Lord is pleased; my soul feels a swift breeze.

See, knowledge is coming forth and we're gaining
wisdom; the mind of Christ, this is my new life.
I gave up that old one and now I'm singing,
speaking bold, coming out pure as gold.
Never say I never I told you so with a strong NO to sin.
Pure Hope, we're entering in and in the end, we will prosper and win.

THE ENEMY WITHIN

I hate it when I give in to smoking.

I come out smelling like smoke, enslaved to an addiction; an
enemy of self pleasing this flesh, that's leading me death.

I pray and plead, crying on my knees; still I find
myself hiding, smoking - full of shame.

It's the enemy within! I need to resist the sin and really let
God into that place, standing on His mercy and grace.

I need to love myself.

I need to conquer and win.

I must give that void of pain to the Most High so I can have a
healthy life, not slowly taking my life with a puff of poison!

I can't blame anybody but myself as I deal with the cause of my actions.

My heart beats fast, my lungs gasp for air how dare I cry!

I'm scared of sin taking my life when righteousness
is supposed to be my new life.

So this day - today -I will take a stand that I
will no longer be an enemy to self.

IT'S A PROCESS

The process may not be easy but sit back and
process what's before your eyes.
Is there something in your way stopping your dreams?
If so, stop screaming and make it happen.
Analyze the situation and seek God's face and He'll show you
why you keep ending up in that same old tired place.

Oh, is it something deep within that you don't want to face?
You're wasting time standing in that same place
of insanity; time will not wait on you.
It's time for you to exam self, confess your sins and face your fears.
Overcome your situation with God's love and
your tears and he'll direct your steps.

When no one believes in you and calls you a fool,
encourage yourself and the master will, too.
You will find you're doing something new with a
renewed mind, elevating further in life.
You will be a testimony that they can make it through any adversities.
Women, we don't have to give our sexuality to men
so we can feel loved or get our bills paid.
Believe in yourself and put an end to that lust
that leads to sexual sin and bondage.

That kind of life will make you feel unhappy,
unloved, with a hardened heart.
See, I know a man that can bring you out of
the dark. His name is Jesus Christ!
You might not believe it only takes faith the size of a mustard seed;
He can save you from self, the enemy within.
What else can you do when that same old tired thing doesn't work?
Try something different and give God a chance and I
promise you, He'll fill that void and never ignore you.
Believe in yourself and try something different.
It won't be easy at first but never give up, and
in the end you will have character.

LOVE HAS CHANGED MY LIFE

When I look at you I see beauty flowing from the
depth of your soul like a clear blue stream.
The love in you is a radiant light that lights up my life.
I watch you loving everything, even your worst enemies.
That kind of love penetrates my heart, making
me think twice, changing my mind.

See, that kind of love surpasses all understanding.
It will affect mankind to ponder, wondering why!
With me, I just cry, saying good bye to that old life.
See, love is so beautiful it has changed my life to the life of Christ, and
I want to share that kind of love with everyone who comes my way.

So I thank the Lord for sending His only begotten
son and sharing his undying love with me.

LaDonna Booker-McLemore

BELIEVE

All things are possible if you have faith and believe; all you
have to do is escape that old mind set and be transformed
by the things that are good, lovely, pure, true and just.

Though the vision tarries wait on it with faith and good works,
knowing the Lord will continue the good work that he started.

For the vision will come to pass, so keep your eyes on the
prize and don't be surprised when it arises, for it comes
from the master who calls us friend. He's omnipotent!

For the kingdom of God is at hand and He's
going to wipe away all the tears.

So stay near and rebuke fear, hearing what
the spirit of the Lord is saying.

Never get weary in doing well and stay prayed
up, seeking His face at all times.

Ask for wisdom and he'll direct your steps.

See, we're one body standing in agreement in one accord, bringing our
gifts and talents to the table, saving souls, knowing we're more than able.

So all we have to do is keep our eyes on Him
and he'll keep us in perfect peace.

This is just to encourage you.

ANOTHER LEVEL OF GREATNESS

I'm going to another level with no fear, forgetting the past, my dear.

Obeying the Most High's voice, knowing I hear.

The Father loves me so much, I shed in tears.

It took me years to release the past; now I'm growing real
fast, doing his will, no longer feeling ill. Living real!

Now I'm giving back, making an attack, letting
this flesh die as my spirit flies high.

I'm giving God my worship and praise because I was
stuck in the haze, living life in a cage full of rage.

I'm now making a stand - Jesus Christ, the only perfect man.

He saved me from my sins, made me a friend, elevating
me to another level of greatness in Him.

BEING COMPLETE IN CHRIST

It's about being complete in Christ, Christ, living a
righteous life, not fighting against the will of God.
The Lord shows us what's in our hearts and we have to go
through a process to become delivered and complete in Him.
We say, "Father, your will be done," then we rebel like the
children of Israel, wandering in the wilderness of our minds
for forty years, never entering the promise land, wanting to
return to Egypt where we were in slavery and bondage.
"That's Insane!"
I want to taste the big sweet grapes, for I'm a giant killer like
David, facing all my fears, making mountains move.

I understand our adversity is all God's plan just like Jesus being
crucified on the cross was a great plan to bring us to a place of
salvation, adopted in the kingdom of God, joint Heirs with Christ,
elevating from glory to glory, maturing in our faith with our Father.
Look, it's about being complete in Christ,
Christ, Christ, living a righteous life.

Oh man of little faith! I want to be a man of great faith like Abraham
who was willing to sacrifice his son, Isaac, accepting God's word,
applying it daily, knowing I am a new creation in Christ and all old
things are passed away. I will press toward the mark of the prize.
You see, I won't look back like Lot's wife, turning into a pillar of salt.
I finally realize my adversities are God's perfect plan for me to become
complete in Christ, so stand steadfast, walking by faith and not sight.
I am complete in Christ, Christ, Christ, living
a holy, righteous, consecrated life.
The father is purging out the leaven of our past to
make us Pure Hope, true Disciples of Christ.
Discern your season and accept His will, stand still, sitting on the
potter's wheel until He molds you into something strong as steel.
I'm going through the fire coming out pure as
gold complete and whole in Christ.

I will enter the land of Canaan, seeing all my hopes and dreams,
praising my king; for he can do the impossible things. Doing my
father's will with character, fishing for souls for the kingdom of
God, leading them to a place of God's grace, letting them know it's
about being dedicated and complete in Christ, Christ, Christ

RAIN

When it rains it pours; one thing I know for sure is God
has opened several doors, so don't be distracted.

When it rains many trails appear; have an ear to
hear. He'll steer you to the right place.

When it rains know that it's blessings you'll
gain; don't get caught living insane.

Move from your comfort zone; it might seem
long. Stand strong; you belong to Christ.

God is opening the flood gates of heaven so let it
rain, and trust in the Lord; he'll sustain you.

Never get weary in doing well; continue working for the Lord
with faith and works and at the end, blessings will manifest.

God knows what time is best, so press; no time for stress. Always confess
as you make your request; He'll fill the void, no more emptiness.

My God is always welcome - my special house guest.

So let it rain, let it rain. Blessings from the Most High I will gain.

NOWADAYS

Nowadays, girls are idolizing the wrong things.

Their minds are on materialistic things,
designer jeans; they want the bling.

They're growing up, shaking their butts, thinking it's
pretty on the television screen; showing it all - not even
knowing God has a calling for their life, eternal life.

Most men have no respect for women.

Blame yourselves, ladies, because young girls are growing up
having low self-esteem, giving in to sexual sin at a young age; now
they're full of rage, always saying, "I can't find a good man!"

Wake up and take a stand.

LaDonna Booker-McLemore

Love yourself; there's nothing better. Christ will
love you forever till the end of time.

Enter His everlasting covenant; it's one of a kind.

Stop blaming men for the things they do; they
only do what you allow them to do!

So stop feeling blue. Christ will guide you through
to the other side if you abide in His will!

No matter what happens; know that you can call on His name, repent,
get it right. Holy Spirit will help you fight while you die to the flesh.

A new life will enter and that old one will vanish and
you'll be a testimony to someone, in Jesus' name.

THANKFUL

I'm thankful, so very thankful to the Lord, for his mercy endures forever.

His mercy is one of a kind, my king who shines like a spotless diamond.

Be thankful at all times; He's the one that designs,
so know it's divine; we're part of the vine. Jesus is
the blood line and we shine because of him.

So be thankful when various adversities come on the
scene; press toward the mark of the prize. It shines like a
beautiful diamond; righteousness is my new life.

The Father will intervene, refining us in the fire of affliction; so count it
all joy, giving God the praise; the enemy can't stand our heavenly voice.

We tear down his plan as we stand knowing that
the trying of our faith opens heaven's gates.

Now let patience have her perfect way as we pray
night and day with a thankful heart.

So give thanks unto the Lord for his mercy is good and endures forever.

Rejoice! I say rejoice, for this is the day the Lord has made. He gave us
life; we're never afraid. Don't get hung up on things that are manmade.

Store your treasures in heavenly things and praise God for our holy king.

So remember, in all things give thanks.

Amen

I NEED THE TRUTH

See, I need the truth, no matter how much it hurts;
it sets me free, blessing me. Then I can see.

The truth helps us to overcome situations; then we can grow.

See, I need the truth; it's the only way I can function and have
good relationships, but a lot of people don't deal with the truth.

To me it's fake!

They want to be your friend; now that's a mistake; they're not
capable of being true to themselves so they can't be true you.

See, they need to be set free by the master and not man, so stand
in the midst of adversities until the breakthrough arises.

Though it's bitter sweet you'll reach your peak; he'll
turn up the heat to make sure you're on beat.

See, I need the truth.

I accept it, willing in my mind, soul, spirit and heart; knowing it
sheds light, casting out the fright as I gain might to elevate in life.

So I thank my heavenly Father for my belt of truth.

The truth that you know will break you free, make you free.

It will unlock doors mentally; bring change in your finances,
relationships, and everything in your environment.

So once again, I need the truth.

SO BLESSED

I am so blessed to have the Father; He's on my side at
all times, being a comforter in my time of need.

See, my Father holds me tight in the midnight hours,
whispering sweetness of love in my ears, giving me peace.

I love the Lord. He's my everything and
without him, I'm alone and nothing!

I will perish without a trace but because of the Messiah
I am so blessed - beyond my wildest dreams.

When I wake up in the morning I'm blessed!

In my coming and going I'm blessed.

I'm so blessed to have a covenant with my heavenly Father.

Amen

ANOTHER LEVEL

I've been elevated to another level and it's
new, but I don't know what to do.
See, I can't step out into the unknown; the fear is not
gone and the Lord tells me that I'm never alone.

I've been elevated to another level, full of all my hopes
and dreams. So tell me why I want to scream?
Like he told me before, I need to elevate my faith and
stop running to my past; I need to escape.

I now understand God has the plan and all I have to do is believe
and stand, knowing that he is not a man and yes, he can.
I know that it's not even me; it's his spirit helping me
to see the blessings that are waiting for me.

So what's the problem, I ask myself?
Then my master shows me that I'm full of fear, trying to put
new wine in old wine skins; that's out of his will; it's a sin.

So now I can enter into his presence all the time,
crying out for help 'cause I want to shine.
I've been elevated to another level; it's his will.
I have no choice but to receive; this is what's real.

I have to step out in faith and let this flesh die. It's
full of lies; it will kill me. I will spiritually die!
I have to escape. I have been elevated.

A REAL MAN

See, I'm waiting for a real man - one that's willing
to stand for the Lord in these perilous days.
His heart is purified and he obeys the Holy Spirit that dwells
in his being; he knows that he belongs to the holy king.

This man will trust in his Father God.
He will worship the Most High on hands and knees and
he's not ashamed; he has been called by his name.

See, this man will worship the Lord in spirit and in truth, being an
example to the dying youth that you don't have to chase females,
knowing that his body is a living sacrifice unto the Lord!

See, I'm looking for a man that worships in the midnight
hour, not letting this world devour his soul.
He stores his treasures in heaven, the real gold.

This man will be a father, a provider, a teacher, a
protector, a developer and a caring one.
He will be the head and not the tail.
He will give and never borrow.
He will pray for this world; it cries with sorrow.
My man of God will love as Christ loves the church.
He will look and smell fine because Christ will shine through him.

He will chase after his dreams and never live in
between, praying and fasting to stay clean.
See, I'm waiting for the Lord to send me that real man.

LaDonna Booker-McLemore

HARD TIMES ARE GOOD

When times are hard will you still praise God?
No job can pay your bills; will you be self-
willed or will you seek, until you find?

You're being polished like a beautiful diamond,
gleaming in this dark world.
When times are hard we have to carry on,
standing strong, suffering with pain.
On today we will reign, being sustained; thank
God for the rain. "I'm still sane!"

When times are hard they're really good, purging us,
correcting us just the way he said it would.
"Dying to this flesh."
When times are hard it's testing our faith.
Will you escape or elevate?

See, we will see our self and the things we need.
God loves us; we're blessed indeed.
So when times are hard, look for the good
because that's how they work out.
So never doubt; praise his name and shout!

Don't give the enemy room; he'll consume trust in the bride groom.
Our praise touches the king. The enemy run and screams.
So obey the Lord when times are hard. It shows our
maturity; he'll bless us with prosperity for eternity.

AS THE RIVER FLOWS

As the river flows my soul cries, yielding myself to Holy
Spirit to show me the way when my eyes cannot see.

My emotions try to take dominion over my life,
making me feel something that's not real.

I'm sharing Christ's sufferings so I can someday reign with him, as I rise
above all situations, walking in love, always trusting in the one above.

See, I know it's not my will or leaning unto my own
understanding because God has a very unique way
of doing things that we cannot understand.

I must stand in faith knowing everything in my life has already
been worked out before He created the foundations of the world.

So I'm resting in His mighty wings, telling him my hopes
and dreams; so as the rivers flow we have to know God
is a present help, always standing by our side.

Remember that God is not a man that He should lie!

We don't have to try; all we have to do is
recognize what is real and what's a lie.

So as the river flows, just know something good
is going to flow in your direction.

So don't ever give up.

LaDonna Booker-McLemore

MY EYES ARE OPEN

Lord, you said ask and it shall be given unto me.

Lord, you said seek and you shall find; you said and the door
shall be opened, and it's not something I'm just hoping.

See, I have faith and it's bigger than the size of a mustard
seed because the Lord has rained down on me; truly indeed
the Lord has blessed me to see another day, to walk in a new
way, a new way. A new creation - that's what I am!

See, I'm starting to see all my hopes and dreams, so I thank my God,
praising my holy king because he can do the impossible things.

God is giving me my heart's desires and it's setting my soul
on fire; he loves me unconditionally, never dissing me; he's
standing by my side. I will praise his name for eternity.

I don't have to pay for my heavenly Father's love or
look for it; it's a gift from heaven above!

God's love surpasses all understanding and His love covers a multitude
of sin, and it enters in, penetrating my heart; and that kind of love
has brought me out of so many things that were full of dark.

My eyes are full of light and I can see, and
my whole body has been set free.

See, my will is now your will and it's not something I'm trying
to feel; I'm just trusting in the one who knows the real.

See, the steps of a good man are ordered by the Lord, taking my
two-edged sword, making my voice heard in these perilous days.

The lord is giving me more - more of His spirit;
and I'm feeling it, and my eyes are open.

LaDonna Booker-McLemore

THE DOOR OF YOUR HEART

The Most High is knocking at the door of your heart,
wanting to give you more - life more abundantly.

Jesus died for you and me so open your eyes and see that faith
the size of a mustard seed can blossom into a beautiful tree.

The key is to believe that you can do all things through Christ.

See, He's knocking at the door of your heart, wanting to give you a new
heart but the choice is yours; it's either going to be your will or His will!

The most High will; he will lead you to His kingdom.

Your will leads you to hell!

Think about it!

WHAT YOU MAKE IT

I used to live a life of shame, playing games, living
insane with no cause, falling with no dignity.

Time was going by; I was full of cry, telling lies with not respect.

See, I was getting older and life was cold, scared to
look at the truth; I was pregnant and a youth.

Then one day I realized I was stuck in the haze, blazing
my mind, my two children were living in crime.

I wanted them to shine and they were so strong but I was long gone.

Then one day Christ opened the door of my heart, telling me
he adores me, giving me the keys that set my soul free.

Now I'm living the life of Christ: baptized and
chastised, with a renewed mind.

See, I'm living life to the fullest, full of self-esteem,
conquering all things, preaching poetic rap to the lost
that life is what you make it through Christ Jesus.

Life is what you make it; the choice is yours.

What are you going to do? Listen to his voice and follow!

All praises go to the holy king, my spirit sings for the
things he did; he taught me how to be an adult, stop
crying and playing games like a school kid.

LaDonna Booker-McLemore

I thank the Lord for his only begotten son, for making
salvation available; that's when my life began.

Jesus, oh how I love that name; he never plays games, he took
away the shame, renewing my mind one day at a time.

See, He made me in his image uniquely, one of a kind.

He was born in a manger; his people treated him like a stranger.

He died on Calvary; think about how sweet it's going
to be when we see our father's glorious face.

We can embrace his holy presence now.

Oh how I love that name; it's not about fame with
you; it's your love that guides me through.

You open my eyes; help me to arise to another level in you that's new.

That's why I love you, Lord: you're building my faith; making
me strong; preparing me for ministry; engrafting me into the
image of Christ; telling me to hold on and have faith; don't live
by sight, but the choice is yours. So what're you going to do?

Listen to his voice and follow through.

MISSION IMPOSSIBLE

Who would give their son to die to save another man's life?

Just take my hand and stand and I'll flow.

Two thousand years ago he steps on the scene to give
eternal life by giving his own, redeeming our souls,
showing us he's the only one in control.

Jesus Christ is his name so stop being distracted
by fame; there's no need to be ashamed.

Mission impossible? I don't think so. I'm going to keep on flowing to
let you know he has made a way for us to see our heavenly Father.

Greater works we shall do if we believe and
we will see his mission completed.

LaDonna Booker-McLemore

See, it's not impossible if you have pure hope!

Just take your place; fall on your knees,
seeking his face, praising his name.

This life is not to be played with; it's the real deal.

Mission impossible? I don't think so. I'll continue to flow.

See, we all have a mission to complete if we let Holy Spirit lead the
way, not listening to what others might say about who we are.

We have to know what God's will is for our life.

So stand strong on his word, and that mission that others
said is impossible will be done, in Jesus name.

I FORGIVE ME

I forgive myself for all I have done; it's time for me to carry on.

It took a long time to release; now I have true belief.

When you don't forgive yourself there's no good health.

So I forgive myself and others, living my life on another level; it's new.

My creator helps me to get better; now I can live with Him forever.

Everlasting life is what the king gave to me when he died
on the tree, giving me the keys that set my soul free.

So once again, I forgive me.

THE REALITY

How could you pretend that you were my friend!

I don't want to mend or spend time with you; we don't blend.
I'm tired of defending myself; we're at a dead end!

You thought you were clever. That's why I'm writing
this letter; however, we will never be together.

You stabbed me in the back with a knife and I was your wife.

You treated me like a low life; now I'm looking for a new life -

A true life, a whole life. Now I'm looking for a new life;

It's about Jesus Christ. He's the one that gave me this life.

I placed you higher than God and wonder why you treated me odd.

See, his love is good; you were only a feel good, falsehood,
no good - not even walking in manhood.

I thought you understood I was messed up because of my
childhood; maybe I was looking for fatherhood!

I withstood all that all you did after you left, playing
games like a school kid, as you backslid.

Then my father told me that unforgiveness
will not make the pain go away.

So I forgive you all day, every day until it all goes away.

I will pray that the Lord will heal you and send you a breakthrough.

Stop running and listen to the still voice.

Father, forgive me for all my sins. Help me to move
forward, using my two-edged sword, never letting
discord step on board; I'm rich and not poor.

I will soar above all things!

I won't fall as long as I keep my eyes on you.

I will look through good eyes.

So I thank you, Father, that I finally realize the reality of your will.

Amen

YOU BLESSED ME

You really blessed me when you left me; now I can see.

I'm discovering who I am from A to Z.

I didn't know I could stand being all that I can be, learning
to love myself unconditionally after you left.

You really blessed me when you left me.

Now I'm standing strong, knowing I belong
to the one who died for my sins.

See, I'm never alone; the past is gone and he calls me
friend till the end. Where he lives is my true home.

See, the Father is never wrong; He sits on the throne. He rules
and reigns; He's the one who brings the change and the rain!

The Most High knows the time; he's the
one that shines; I'm looking fine.

I live because of Him; I move and have my
being. He's the air that I breathe.

Every day, every hour and moment, God is all that and all things!

See, the Lord really blessed me when I thought the one
thing that I really, really, really needed left me.

LOST AND FOUND

Being a single mother father never bothers, full of
rage single-minded, on the wrong page.

Children asking where is dad; confused, he's dead!

Mom telling lies to get by saying "Hi" to the wrong man, waiting.
The phone - you gave it up, now he's long gone. You're left alone

Now you're really mad, barely getting by, getting high
as your children cry; you just want to die.

See, I know a man that will come into your heart.

He'll take away the pain and help you rise above the rain; his name is
Jehovah Jireh, your provider; he's the Great I Am when no one else can.

King of Kings, Lord of Lords, all you need to do is get on board of
his holy ship and sail away; he died for our sins he made a way.

Now leave the past and enter the future.

It's nothing to it but to do it.

LaDonna Booker-McLemore

With faith, hope, love all things are possible; without
a doubt, he's the one who brought me out.

Now I'm spreading the Father's word in a unique way.

See, I was that woman above; now I'm giving much love
to my hurting, lost sisters and even the hookers.

That the lifestyle you live is to blame.

Give your life to the master - no more shame.

He's the king that rules and reigns.

I once was lost but by the grace of God I have been
found; gave up my life and he turned it all around.

He's giving me a new life full of hopes and dreams.

I will see my master because I answered the call and I'm obedient.

BEAUTIFUL VIRTUOUS WOMAN

Bishop Mariea Claxton, you are truly a beautiful virtuous vessel full of the word of God, educating his disciples, helping them to stand strong in the midst of any situation with unconditional love.

Bishop, you have an awesome concern for the body of Christ and the Most High is directing you to help us mature to another level in Him by spending time laboring with us.

Your Bible teachings should not be taken for granted because our lives will truly change as the word stimulates our minds into being transformed; the shackles and chains are loosed!

Now we have a new way of thinking - the way He does.

God is unfolding himself to us in all our teachings and we are starting to take our place, being on one accord and everything will flow as planned.

Bishop, you are standing so strong and not concerning yourself with the things of this world.

LaDonna Booker-McLemore

You are concerned about heavenly things as your
spirit softly sings sweetness of joy and peace.

When I'm going through obstacles in my life, Bishop,
you minister to me and I come out feeling new,
walking in everything that God has for me.

A covenant with God is what is being presented to me and my
soul screams because God has sent his holy king, and all the
impossible things become possible as I walk into all my dreams.

So I thank God for blessing me with an obedient leader
who teaches me leadership to do His will.

Pure Hope has been blessed with a special
gift; a beautiful virtuous vessel!

HAVE AMBITION

We can get on a spiritual level where we don't allow any
mess to be injected into our thought life; knowing that
when he died on the tree it was all said and done.

So why are we wresting with all those old things?

See, we're uneducated, feeding our old man, going
in circles, playing insane mind games.

We let our emotions guide us to notions, drinking the
wrong potion of the enemy, not taking up our cross daily
or listening to the boss who knows what's best; forgetting
the rest; and we wonder why we're so stressed!

See, we're holding onto the mess; it's our comfort zone, zoning
out, selling out one another instead of being on one accord.

I'm getting tired; I'm getting bored with the same old mess.

I'm taking my two- edged sword, flowing these lyrics.

Holy Spirit is showing me what's real!

See, I can't waste time; it won't wait on me; swiftly being
diligent instead of thinking on what made me mad or sad.

I'm now applying the word of God, forgiving my enemies
because it was said and done on the cross.

Jesus is the boss, my scape goat, so get on His level and power we
will see, and it will be hard for any man to disrespect you or me.

I turn the cheek in many aspects, expecting me to give into my flesh!

I'm making a stand for righteousness; it's now part of my
niche; not worrying about gossip because my words elevate
mankind to stand up and shine in these perilous days.

So many people are stuck in a daze, and the haze is their reality.

I'm praying for the lost; I don't want them to get caught up in the blaze.

I'm getting ready, steady suffering with pain so I can someday reign;
being crushed, my anointing is getting strong to do his perfect will.

The Lord has given me ambition and nothing can stop me now.

I have no excuse why I'm not doing His will; I will stand doing all I
can and God's perfect plan will come to pass with mercy and grace.

So have ambition.

ENJOYING LIFE TO THE FULLEST

Enjoying life to the fullest, doing my Father's will, full of all my dreams.

I enjoy my job; I work for the king!

There's no one better than him who brings fulfillment into my life.

God is pulling all that's within me out and
prosperity, joy are coming forth.

See, it's not about me; it's the greater one who lives inside
helping me to do the will of God as I yield myself.

As I walk down the road God reveals to me His provision for the day.

So keep your ears and eyes open

So you won't miss the mark of the prize.

Now the steps of a good man are ordered by the Lord.

I'm a good man, so I will watch and stand.

God is not a man that he can lie, and his word will
not come back void without accomplishing.

See, I'm enjoying life to the fullest, worshipping my Father in spirit and
in truth, knowing the difference between natural and spiritual things.

It's not about this life; it's about living like Christ and eternal things.

Now you must stay sober at all times, storing your
treasures in the right place - heaven.

LaDonna Booker-McLemore

WISDOM AND TRUTH

Wisdom and truth can take you far in life but we choose to go through
instead of asking for wisdom from our Father who knows all things.

At times we act as if we can make it without him; that's
how we get caught up, walking in insanity.

When our Father puts the truth before us, we can't reject it!

We must man-up and deal with the hurt and
the pain of the truth; it set's us free.

If we want better insight and discernment in our lives, we must learn
to reverence the Most High and put our trust in him at all times.

We need to listen to wisdom and treasure her; she knows
the outcome when we make good or bad decisions.

So when going through all one must do is call on his name,
and then apply the wisdom of God, which is his word!

So on today if you have not received Jesus Christ
as Lord and Savior, you will lack wisdom.

If you accept Christ, it's the first step toward wisdom and truth.

THE PATH OF LIFE

Life can lead you down several trails; however, we
have to apply knowledge to gain wisdom.

Then we will go down the right path.

Lust can lead mankind into various dysfunctional
relationships that cause anger, sickness and craziness.

Accepting Christ can lead you to wholeness, love, prosperity and eternity.

The choices we make in life set our destiny;
it kills me to see my people fall.

Stand tall for something that matters no matter what it costs.

Give up yourself; trust in someone else that
knows best and shows us how to rest.

See, his unconditional love makes life hopeful with no shame.

He never plays games, always remaining the same.

Life can lead you down several paths.

It can be spiritual death or life! The choice is yours.

Money, drugs and sex look so good but everything that
looks good may be deceiving you out of time.

So unwind and spend time with the Father in these perilous days.

LaDonna Booker-McLemore

TRIALS & TRIBULATIONS

You don't know what I've been through, you don't know my pain; after I flow. These lyrics are going to make all my enemies look ashamed.

Trials and tribulations, people hating, waiting, calculation; they don't know the time rewind!

See, it's my destiny; no man can stop me. I'm free; they're low key. He takes me through the Red Sea.

I come out smelling like potpourri, carefree. Look and see I love like Christ; it's his righteousness that gives me life.

Now I'm going to another level, fighting like a rebel for sure.

He's knocking at the door of your heart; it's a new start, so depart from that old life - low life, thug life - to eternal life.

Live a true life, an abundant life, a whole life with no strife; through Christ.

Now the choice is yours.

Either or; we will sit before the Holy King who judges all things. His Father knows all things.

I'm not here to pacify; I'm here to prophesy with a spiritual eye.

His love multiplies, taking me high; can't understand why he loves me so much when I cry, letting this flesh die; He's taking me high.

I'm going to see my dream even though it tarries.

I never get weary 'cause I keep my eyes on the king and not the bling.

Stop playing game; you're living in-between!

See, He's my everything; I'm a royal priestess,
keeping it clean when I sing.

The world's music needs a vaccine.

It's destroying the younger generation's minds.

The enemy is trying to take your peace, I'm fighting for mine.

We have to pray for the world; lost boys and girls are losing
their minds when they should be shining for Christ.

See, we're living in the last days full of crime with trials and tribulations.

THE WAGES OF SIN IS DEATH!

It's time out playing around with sin.

We need to enter into God's presence, seeking his
face, understanding that we need to get in place, in
order to win this spiritual race that's before us.

If we want good fruit our trees must be planted on good
ground; water with the word so our roots can grow deep.

See, I want to be like that tree planted by rivers of water.

I shall not be moved, moved by any situation or respond out of
this flesh but respond according to the fruit of the spirit.

Applying the word daily is a must, no time to lust!

It's time out for playing around with sin, for the wages
of sin is death - nothing more, nothing less.

It's full of mess; we have to understand who we are in Christ.

Then we will be able to move forth in the things of God.

"For the kingdom of God is at hand"

We have to stand, doing all we can to stand, trusting
in the only one who died for our sins.

Jesus is our scapegoat and we have to know that we are new
creations in Christ, reconciled to our heavenly Father.

HOW LONG?

How long will you carry on with living beneath you privileges?

You can't pay your bills, self-willed, standing still, going
downhill; feeding your flesh so it can feel good.

He gives us free will but until you submit to his will
the visions he gave you will never be fulfilled!

We're a royal priesthood, a holy nation, and joint heirs with Christ.

How long will you walk in fear?

Who do you fear? You need to adhere to Holy
Spirit, make an atmosphere and draw near.

The Most High will steer your steps and
make it all clear; you'll persevere!

How long will you let sin hinder your blessings?

Smoking nicotine, can't even sing, you're living in-between;
let the Most High intervene; the flesh screams, it's clean.

You're no longer a juvenile; reconcile - it's worthwhile.

Christ will look and smile; He'll give you a new lifestyle -holy.

VALIDATION

Don't we all need confirmation, elevation, revelations
in all situations, but it has to be God-sent!

As long as God validates your dreams, let no man tell you
otherwise; look through spiritual eyes; they never lie.

See, Holy Spirit ratifies what is true when the
world is coming down on you.

Stand unmovable; confirmation comes to the scene, its
various things. Don't miss the gleam; it shines like bling.
Praise the holy king when you're feeling blue.

It's the sweet-smelling armor going to heavenly places.

Yes, he's pleased indeed.

God knows what's in a man's heart and he will
reveal to us our mess by his spirit.

See, he wants to guide us to a brand-new level in Him; so
let no man condemn what you're going through.

I just pray, making my request and the Father validates the rest;
He knows what's best and in the end, V-I-C-T-O-R-Y we win.

LOVE

Love, what is love?

Is it your heart pounding when you see that special loved
one or is it enduring the trials in a relationship?

Love, what is love?

Is it giving your sexuality to an individual or is it respecting
each other's temples until holy matrimony?

Love, what is love?

Is it you saying nice things to make others feel good or is
it telling someone the truth and setting them free?

Love, what is love?

Some people mistake lust for love; how to know the differences?

Lust only lasts for the act, and love is patient, love is kind, love is
loving your worst enemies; love is obedient to the will of God!

Love is truthful and positive when you're feeling
low; just trust in the Most High.

See, God is love and he gave his only begotten son so we can become
redeemed and have dreams, singing in his holy presence for eternity.

What is love?

Love is giving my all, taking a stand for righteousness.

LaDonna Booker-McLemore

LOVE-VS-LUST

Lust is a must; it consumes, feeling good for a minute or two and after you're through you're feeling blue – crying, not knowing what to do!

Girl, if you want true love, love yourself; there's nothing better.

Treat yourself like a queen; you don't have to
scream. Just praise the holy king.

Get yourself together; write yourself a mental letter, so when that wolf comes dressed in sheep clothes, you'll have your noise wide open.

So don't take the bait; you know it's fake. Escape.

Love-vs-lust

Love is not a feeling. It's something you give, not a
nigga splitting your wig, treating you like a pig!

Love is long suffering like never before.

He opens the door, never treats you like a whore.

Love wants to give you more; love conquers all things.

Lust will have you going in circles, tripping out, without a doubt.

True love will bring you out of any situation when people hate.

Love believes in all things, it never schemes; it
loves the crack fiends into having dreams.

Love-vs-lust

Lust will have you disgusted, up in a rut, head
in your butt because you got cut!

You'll be stressing, never dressing, pressing
toward depression without a question.

Love-vs-lust

Lust is not the answer; it's true love from heaven above.

TRUE LOVE

I wonder how it feels.

I never had it; I know it's real. True love!

I want someone to feel my heart and give back the
passion I so desire that my soul requires.

I want somebody to understand my emotional needs.

I'm an emotional being.

I have heard and seen this thing called love that
I so desire, that my soul requires.

See, it sets my soul on fire and I don't want to retire
this desire that always seem to backfire.

I really admire seeing two on one accord.

With a beautiful conversation, no frustration or
fornication; building a strong foundation with God's
confirmation till death do us part, no cancellation.

See, desperation kicks in to make it work when it's the creator's will.

I feel a chill; it's not a cheap thrill. The Lord will fulfill this true
love that my soul requires. He's not a man; the enemy is a liar.

True love will grow from friendship, to courtship
then partnership; it never quits.

The Lord of Hosts will equip when lying lips try to speak
corrupt, to break up what God has joined together.

True love will stand when times are longsuffering.

True love will get up, build up and line up
with the principles of His word.

True love comes from heaven above, singing like a blue bird.

God will receive all the glory in the end; this world is full of sin.

We're praying for one another, never letting it in; we're spiritual kin.

So I thank my Father for this love that I so desire, that my soul requires.

ONLY GOD'S LOVE

No more money, no more drugs, no more thugs; only God's love.

It will remain the same when your friends walk away.

The Father is making a way when we can't see.

I pray that this seed will penetrate your heart and soul;
then the love of God will blossom and unfold.

I'm praying for a renewed mind, the mind of Christ.

It will transform your life into the life of Christ!

Only the love of God can heal that man and
help him to stand for righteousness.

God will deal with that man's heart that's full of
fear and anger that turned into pain.

His soul and land need to be set free from this world that
makes him bold in a way that no man can enter in.

Only God's love can tear down the strongholds that
the enemy placed in his mind and life.

You can have materialistic things such as cars, bling, houses and
all the fine clothes and still feel alone, dying inside, full of pride.

See, God's love is there waiting for us to embrace.

All we have to do is enter into his holy presence.

So when you're feeling depressed, hopeless, wanting to
end it all, attempt to give his undying love a chance.

I promise you that giving your life to him, going through all
your long suffering and trusting in Him, you will arrive.

See, this is not a coincidence; it's an opportunity
to bring you to your destiny.

This is not random; he has handpicked you when
this world will overlook you; it's his will!

Water that seed of love that has pierced your heart; you'll overcome.

Come out of the dark!

We all long for His love; that's our greatest desire, but we don't
know until it blossoms and we choose the greatest love of all:

Jesus Christ.

LaDonna Booker-McLemore

VISION

I have a vision in my mind that seems impossible to me.

Lord, you say ask and it shall be given unto me; faith the size
of a mustard seed can blossom into a beautiful tree.

You must believe that all things are possible.

The Lord gives us all a vision to fulfill but without a vision the
people will perish and without a people there is no vision.

So write the vision down and God will make it
plain for you to see with spiritual eyes.

Then you've got to step out, not knowing what direction you're
going in, and the Lord will be a light guiding your steps.

Though the vision will tarry, wait on it in faith, doing all
you can to stand as the raging storms of life come.

Rise above it all, knowing that God is not a man that he should lie.

For the vision is for an appointed time that only God
knows, and it will come to pass in its seasons.

After you suffer a while you will become strong, established,
patient; and you'll become complete and whole in Christ.

So no matter what comes your way, know that you're blessed.

Look at the good things in your life and others as
well and you'll see God's mercy and grace.

Know that the Most High is working right now in your life
because he first loved us and sent His only begotten son.

Abundant life is what he's presenting, so always
remember that God has given you a vision.

WHO IS?

Father, you are everything to me - my dream!

You have awakened and taken away all my sins; delivered me within.

You have poured your longsuffering love, full
of hope so pure into my heart.

I'm so honored to have you as my daddy; never
forsaking me but increasing me.

"I give glory to your name."

Your love goes so deep and is so wide, my spirit sings Hallelujah!

Who is like the Lord of Hosts?

You're excellent in battle; your majesty reigns forever.

Father, you are the light of my life and the whole
world, opening blind eyes to see spiritually, unlocking
the deaf ears to hear your precious voice.

Who is like the Lord? Who's willing to give his
only begotten son to die for our sins?

No one is able to reconcile man unto the Lord but
you Father God, through your beloved son.

So once again, who is like the Lord that provides, protects, heals, gives
shelter, and delivers us, loving us unconditionally, and calls us friend?

No one.

HE'S BUILDING ME STRONG

He's building up this temple, making me strong.

He's encouraging me every day to hold on to all my hopes and dreams.

He's the holy king who knows all things; when things
may seem as though they will never come to pass.

I look with spiritual eyes, knowing otherwise,
pressing toward the mark of the prize.

He's building up this temple.

It's his amazing grace that I will see the Lord face to face.

It's because of his unconditional love.

I will never put anything above my Father; he always bothers.

I'm never alone, and when I fall off, he carries me on;
there's only one set of footprints in the sand.

Jesus is the holy man who died for my sins; now I
can enter the most holy place in the spirit.

He's building up this temple, making me strong, preparing me for
ministry; and the world will see that he dwells on the inside.

Greater works in these perilous times we
shall do, fighting spiritual crimes.

See, I'm elevating from glory to glory unto the day of
Christ's coming; it's part of His will and for real.

LaDonna Booker-McLemore

COMFORT ZONE

One day I woke up and realized that I was in a place and couldn't move.
This has been a place that I have been in for a very long time,
No matter how hard I tried to move away from the things
I've always known - even the dysfunctional ones.
See, I needed a renewed mind to bring my
thoughts under subjection to Holy Spirit.
I had to discipline my thoughts to think on positive
things, things my flesh didn't want to do.
I had to learn to love newness - treasuring it, trusting
my Father, knowing He will help me through.

I woke up one day and realized I was in a comfort
zone and it was destroying my life.
See, God is always taking us to new levels, and a
comfort zone will stop you right in your tracks.
It's not in God's plan for us to become comfortable; that's why He
tells us that He will continue the good work he started in us.
So I have to press, never giving up doing my Father's will.
So if you have been in a place for a very long time, knowing
that it's time to move to the next level in your life,
No matter what your environment is saying, press toward
all your dreams, even if you can't see the landmark.
The Most High will direct your steps if you have faith and step out.
Get to know God and what he is doing for you right at
this moment; focus and meditate on His word.
See, I woke up one day and realized I was delivered.

LIFE IN THE HOOD

Life in the hood can be good if we learn to
stick together the way we should.

Everywhere I look in the hood is off the hook.

It's black on black crime; who has the biggest bling and rims that shine?

You can't even walk a straight line, selling your people rocks and dimes.

Oh, we're living in the last days for sure.

Revelations unfolding, we're living in war; it's coming to pass too fast.

See, life is cold; the youth are bold, taking one another's lives.
It really bites seeing my people fight, living thug life.

They don't have a clue; we need to stick together like glue
in these perilous days, fighting spiritual crimes.

Where is the faith?

We need to escape the poverty in the mind; it's full of waste.

In the hood it's heisting, hating, faking and selling out your brother.

Children lacking fathers; they never bother.

LaDonna Booker-McLemore

We're falling in the hood, never looking at what's good.

Life in the hood can be good if we learn to
stick together the way we should.

Our communities are full of wealth but we can't see,
tearing down one another when one gets their degree.

There's so much talent going to waste; girl give
me that (sex) is such a disgrace.

So what if we were sold, beat and shackled in chains.

That was the past; we have been set free not by
man, but by the blood of the lamb.

So stop wasting time about what somebody owes you!

Jesus Christ will usher you into a new life.

See, life in the hood can be good if we learn
to stick together the way we should.

For men, does it make you feel like a man to carry heat?

Now you're in up to your knees deep!

Letting your emotions guide your feet.

Now you're on the streets getting beat, as you kept
the heat that made you weep in the first place!

Mud on your face, stuck like paste; look at your soul waste.

Thank God that He gives us new mercy and grace each and every day.

Life is incomplete without our creator, God Almighty.

Life in the hood can be good if we learn to
stick together the way we should.

LIFE

Life, life, life; thug life, hard knock life, spiritual life,
eternal life, life of crime, life work, lifesaving, life-less.

Life is given, life is taken away and what is done from the beginning
to the end can be filled with laughter and pain; but without
acknowledging Christ, life passes away with very little meaning.

For this journey called life will take its course, and we must utilize our
time aspiring toward our vision, because time doesn't wait for anybody.

Life is what you make it; it's a choice.

See, you must walk in faith, never allowing your
environment to dictate who you are.

Stand strong knowing the calling God has for you.

It's a special plan that no man can take away
if you believe all things are possible.

So have big dreams, and the holy king shall bring it to pass.

Life, life, life; thug life, hard knock life, spiritual life, life-less.

What is life when we were made from the ground; he breathed and we fell down; then Jesus came down, redeeming the lost.

Now we have a cause; it's part of the master plan.

Understand that God is not a man; he's the creator of life, of faith that lives in me, giving me abundantly, setting me free to enjoy life to the fullest.

So take your place and press your way until you make it.

See, it's not a dream; sing praise to the king.

One thing I do know is this life will soon pass away and I will live for eternity because I'm obedient.

MY LITTLE ANGELS

A gift from heaven above, full of such love; I want ever take you for granted. I remember you giving me a hug, picking me a flower, or making me a picture that's full of love. Oh how special and dear you all are to me, in spite of my mistakes the Lord blessed me with two beautiful, amazing children that's full of hope and love.

Who could of imagine that a child so little could be so big and strong; strong enough to help me hold on to life. my special gifts from heaven above that loves me no matter mistakes I make. In my corner at all times when I'm going through; I love you mommy makes everything brand new.

Praying for me to stand strong, to do all I can as we walk together down this journey called life. I will continue imparting the wisdom of God into your lives. I will treasure my little angels from heaven above; Jamil and LaTelle, I will love you till death do us part and thereafter.

FATHER'S DAY IS EVERYDAY

My birth father, he doesn't even bother!

My heavenly Father cares about all my needs,
chastening, baptizing in His holy fire.

He had to take away all the sexual sin that got implanted deep within.

He had to teach me a new way to love myself the way He
does, not trying any voodoo to get the love I desire.

Only my heavenly Father can teach me what
my biological father was lacking.

See, it wasn't his fault; it was a generational curse.

The Most High allowed me to break it all, delivering
me, standing tall, not giving my body to a man!

I was disgracing myself; now I'm letting you, oh Lord, take
the place that was filled with so much lust and waste.

My Father is a daddy on every day; I'm honoring,
praising, and worshipping His holy name.

This world only honors fathers once a year.

Sometimes I have to shed a tear, for every year, He's standing so near.

I never have to step to the rear but tap and
plug into his presence, my dear.

See, the things he has for me are more than I can imagine or see.

LaDonna Booker-McLemore

Jesus loves me so much that I allowed Him to come into my heart.

His unconditional love has brought me out of the dark!

Now I have light and I can see; my soul and mind have been set free.

His healing power is spreading from head to
toe; no man can shut the door.

It's a new beginning!

Slavery sins, that's the end, and I will never forget the day
I let you into my life; see it will never be the same.

Heaven is the place I want to relate - only love, no hate.

The white pearly gates and the streets of gold;
that old life was so ugly and cold.

Now I'm resting in my Father's arms until I fall asleep.

No man (only my Daddy) can fill the void that was destroying me.

You see my Father is a daddy every day, correcting me, never
leaving me, and directing me down the right path.

He will receive all the glory in my life because
without him I'm alone and nothing.

So reconnect with your Holy Father and exchange
your old ugly life for the life of Christ.

ABOUT THE AUTHOR

LaDonna McLemore was born on February 22, 1976 as a twin to Dianne and Jerry Booker, in Inkster, Michigan. Chaos and rejection caused her to have no self-worth and at nineteen she was a broken mother of two beautiful children. LaDonna found herself in an abusive relationship for several years; not knowing what real love was.

Life would continue beating her down and she start seeking God for help. In 1998, LaDonna accepted Jesus Christ as her savor. She attended Eagle's Way Full Gospel Ministries. Poetry is LaDonna; she discovered her talents through adversities of life. LaDonna received her GED and studied at Wayne County Community College; also gaining other trades. She's perusing her dreams as an entrepreneur. LaDonna is married to Harold McLemore. They reside in Detroit, Michigan with their three smaller children. The journey of LaDonna has healed and strength her mentally. Her motto has been "giving up is not an option."

SYNOPSIS

Elevating Purpose is a compilation of poetry that speaks volumes of truth. This book deals with unresolved issues fear, lack, etc. that occurs daily; blinding the essence of our true nature. This book is a reflection of LaDonna's journey seeking truth and freedom. The seed of faith has blossomed Elevating purpose.